[This book is intentionally blank!]

[This book is intentionally blank!]

[This book is intentionally blank!]

[This book is intentionally blank!]

[This book is intentionally blank!]

[This book is intentionally blank!]

[This book is intentionally blank!]

[This book is intentionally blank!]

[This book is intentionally blank!]

[This book is intentionally blank!]

[This book is intentionally blank!]

[This book is intentionally blank!]

[This book is intentionally blank!]

[This book is intentionally blank!]

[This book is intentionally blank!]

[This book is intentionally blank!]

[This book is intentionally blank!]

[This book is intentionally blank!]

[This book is intentionally blank!]

[This book is intentionally blank!]

[This book is intentionally blank!]

[This book is intentionally blank!]

[This book is intentionally blank!]

[This book is intentionally blank!]

[This book is intentionally blank!]

[This book is intentionally blank!]

[This book is intentionally blank!]

[This book is intentionally blank!]

[This book is intentionally blank!]

[This book is intentionally blank!]

[This book is intentionally blank!]

[This book is intentionally blank!]

[This book is intentionally blank!]

[This book is intentionally blank!]

[This book is intentionally blank!]

[This book is intentionally blank!]

[This book is intentionally blank!]

[This book is intentionally blank!]

[This book is intentionally blank!]

[This book is intentionally blank!]

[This book is intentionally blank!]

[This book is intentionally blank!]

[This book is intentionally blank!]

[This book is intentionally blank!]

[This book is intentionally blank!]

[This book is intentionally blank!]

[This book is intentionally blank!]

[This book is intentionally blank!]

[This book is intentionally blank!]

[This book is intentionally blank!]

[This book is intentionally blank!]

[This book is intentionally blank!]

[This book is intentionally blank!]

[This book is intentionally blank!]

[This book is intentionally blank!]

[This book is intentionally blank!]

[This book is intentionally blank!]

[This book is intentionally blank!]

[This book is intentionally blank!]

[This book is intentionally blank!]

[This book is intentionally blank!]

[This book is intentionally blank!]

[This book is intentionally blank!]

[This book is intentionally blank!]

[This book is intentionally blank!]

[This book is intentionally blank!]

[This book is intentionally blank!]

[This book is intentionally blank!]

[This book is intentionally blank!]

[This book is intentionally blank!]

[This book is intentionally blank!]

[This book is intentionally blank!]

[This book is intentionally blank!]

[This book is intentionally blank!]

[This book is intentionally blank!]

[This book is intentionally blank!]

[This book is intentionally blank!]

[This book is intentionally blank!]

[This book is intentionally blank!]

[This book is intentionally blank!]

[This book is intentionally blank!]

[This book is intentionally blank!]

[This book is intentionally blank!]

[This book is intentionally blank!]

[This book is intentionally blank!]

[This book is intentionally blank!]

[This book is intentionally blank!]

[This book is intentionally blank!]

[This book is intentionally blank!]

[This book is intentionally blank!]

[This book is intentionally blank!]

[This book is intentionally blank!]

[This book is intentionally blank!]

[This book is intentionally blank!]

[This book is intentionally blank!]

[This book is intentionally blank!]

[This book is intentionally blank!]

[This book is intentionally blank!]

Made in the USA
Coppell, TX
08 February 2022

73166000R00059